PHOTOGRAPHS BY Nathan Farb

Galápagos

INTRODUCTION BY Barry Lopez

COMMENTARY BY Michael H. Jackson

RIZZOLI NEW YORK

FRONTISPIECE:
Panorama of Sulivan Bay, off the island
of Santiago, viewed from Bartolomé.

First published in the United States of America in 1989 by
RIZZOLI INTERNATIONAL PUBLICATIONS, INC.
300 Park Avenue South, New York, NY 10010

Library of Congress Cataloging-in-Publication Data

Farb, Nathan, 1941—
Galápagos/photographs by Nathan Farb; introduction
by Barry Lopez; commentary by Michael H. Jackson.
    p.   cm.
  ISBN 0 – 8478 – 1120 – 4
    1. Galápagos Islands—Description and travel—1981—
—Views. 2. Natural history—Galápagos Islands—Pictorial
works. I. Lopez, Barry Holstun, 1945—   . II. Jackson,
Michael H. (Michael Hume), 1959—   . III. Title.
F3741.G2F37   1989   89–45425
986.6'5 — dc20   CIP

ISBN 0–8478–1120–4

For
Dorothy Little
Rae Feldman
Jeanette Horwich
Lee Marks
Davidine Steele
Adele Saxe
Norma May

DESIGNED BY Nai Y. Chang
TYPESET BY David E. Seham Associates, Inc., Metuchen, New Jersey
PRINTED AND BOUND BY Amilcare Pizzi, S.p.A., Milan, Italy

Contents

Galápagos

PINTA
(Abington)

MARCHENA
(Bindloe)

GENOVESA
(Tower)

Darwin Bay

Prince Phillip's Steps

Roca Redonda

Punta Albemarle

Volcán Ecuador

Volcán Wolf

Cape Berkeley

Punta Vicente Roca

Banks Bay

Volcán Darwin

James Bay

SANTIAGO
(James, San Salvador)

Buccaneer Cove

Cerro Inn

Sulivan Bay

Bolívar Channel

Puerto Egas

Punta Espinosa

BARTOLOMÉ

SEYMOUR
(North Seymour)

Tagus Cove

Sugarloaf

Pinnacle Rock

FERNANDINA
(Narborough)

RÁBIDA
(Jervis)

Bainbridge Rocks

BALTRA
(South Seymour)

Urvina Bay

DAPHNE

Volcán La Cumbre

Volcán Alcedo

Perry Isthmus

Cerro Crocker

Puntudo

PLAZAS

Gemelos

Elizabeth Bay

Cartago Bay

Media Luna

PINZÓN
(Duncan)

Charles Darwin
Research Station

Tortuga Bay

Academy Bay

Volcán Chico

SANTA CRUZ
(Indefatigable)

SANTA FÉ
(Barrington)

Volcán Sierra Negra

Volcán Santo Tomás

ISABELA
(Albemarle)

Puerto Ayora

Cerro Azul

Puerto Villamil

Punta Essex

TORTUGA

Devil's Crown

Punta Cormorant

Post Office Bay

PACIFIC OCEAN

FLOREANA
(Charles, Santa María)

GARDNER

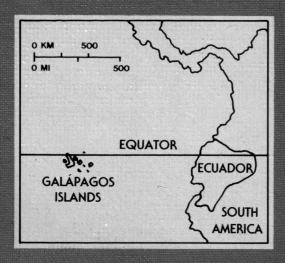

O KM 500
O MI 500

EQUATOR

GALÁPAGOS
ISLANDS

ECUADOR

SOUTH
AMERICA

Most geographical designations in the Galápagos have several variants, both Spanish and English. Those indicated are the names in common usage. Frequently used variants are given in parentheses.

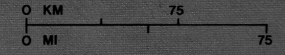

O KM 75
O MI 75

Stephens Bay

SAN CRISTÓBAL
(Chatham)

Puerto Baquerizo Moreno

N

Gardner Bay

ESPAÑOLA
(Hood)
Punta
Suarez

Life and Death in Galápagos

BY BARRY LOPEZ

Fog, melancholy as a rain-soaked dog, drifts through the highlands, beading my hair with moisture. On the path ahead a vermilion flycatcher, burning scarlet against the muted greens of the cloud forest, bursts up in flight. He flies to a space just over my head and flutters there furiously, an acrobatic stall, a tiny, wild commotion that hounds me down the muddy trail, until I pass beyond the small arena of his life. Soon another comes and leaves; and afterward another, tiny escorts on a narrow trail descending the forest.

I had not expected this, exactly. The day before, down below at the airstrip, I'd looked out over a seared lava plain at the thin, desultory cover of leafless brush and thought *in this slashing light there will be no peace.* How odd now, this damp, cool stillness. Balsa and *Scalesia* trees, festooned with liverworts and mosses, give on to stretches of grassland where tortoises graze. Blue-winged teal glide the surface of an overcast pond. The migrant fog opens on a flight of doves scribing a rise in the land; and then, like sliding walls, it seals them off.

Beneath this canopy of trees, my eyes free of the shrill burden of equatorial light, my cheeks cool as the underside of fieldstone—I had not thought a day like this would come in Galápagos. I had thought, foolishly, only of the heat-dunned equator, of a remote, dragon-lair archipelago in the Pacific. I had been warned off any such refreshing scenes as these by what I had read. Since 1535 chroniclers have made it a point to mark these islands down as inhospitable, deserted stone blisters in a broad ocean, harboring no wealth of any sort. A French entrepreneur, M. de Beauchesne-Gouin, dismissed them tersely (and typically) in 1700: *la chose du monde la plus affreuse,* the most horrible place on Earth. Melville, evoking images of holocaust and despair in *The Encantadas,* viewed the Galapagean landscape as the aftermath of a penal colony. A visiting scientist wrote in 1924 that Isla Santa Cruz, where I now wandered, "made Purgatory look like the Elysian Fields."

Sea lions rest on the lava rocks border-
ing the lagoon on the island of Santa
Fé, where the prickly pear cactus, usually a low-growing plant, has developed a trunk and grown to tree size.

OVERLEAF:
Sesuvium vegetation, red during the
dry season, is interspersed with prickly
pear on the island of South Plaza.

Obviously, I reflected, feeling the heft of the mist against
the back of my hands and the brightness of bird song around
me, our summaries were about to differ. And it was not solely
because these writers had never ventured far inland, away
from the bleak coasts. Singularly bent to other tasks—commercial exploitation, embroidering on darkness in a literary narra-
tive, compiling names in the sometimes inimical catalogs of
science—they had rendered the islands poorly for a visitor in-
tent, as I was, on its anomalies, which by their irreducible contrariness reveal, finally, a real landscape.

Galápagos, an archipelago of thirteen large and six smaller islands and some forty exposed rocks and islets, occupies a por-
tion of the eastern Pacific half the size of Maine. It lies on the
equator, but oddly; the Humboldt Current, flowing up from the
Antarctic Ocean, has brought penguins to live here amidst tropical fish, but its coolness inhibits the growth of coral; and the
freshwater streams and sandy beaches of, say, equatorial Cura-
çao or Martinique are not to be found here. The Galápagos are
black shield volcanos, broadly round massifs that rise symetrical-
ly to collapsed summits, called calderas. Their lightly vegetated
slopes incline like dark slabs of grit to cactus-strewn plains of
lava. The plains, a lay of rubble like a storm-ripped ocean frozen at midnight, run to precipitous coasts of gray basalt, where
one finds, occasionally, a soothing strip of mangrove. Reptiles
and birds, the primitive scaled and feathered alone, abound
here; no deer-like, no fox-like, no hare-like animal abides.
  The tendency to dwell on the barrenness of the lowlands,
and on the seeming reptilian witlessness of the tortoise, as
many early observers did, to diminish the landscape cavalierly
as an "inglorious panorama"—an ornithologist's words—of Cre-
taceous beasts, was an inevitability, perhaps; but the notion
founders on more than just the cloud forests of Santa Cruz.
Pampas below many of the islands' calderas roll like English
downs serenely to the horizon. Ingenious woodpecker finches
pry beetle grubs from their woody chambers with cactus spines.
The dawn voice of the dove is as plaintive here as in the streets
of Cairo or São Paulo. Galápagos, the visitor soon becomes
aware, has a kind of tenderness about it; its stern vulcanism,
the Age of Dragons that persists here, eventually comes to
seem benign rather than aberrant. That nobility that occasionally marks a scarred human face gleams here.
  Biologists call Galápagos "exceptional" and "truly extraordinary" among the world's archipelagos. They pay homage to its
heritage by referring to it as "the Mt. Sinai of island biogeogra-
phy." But these insular landscapes give more than just scientific,

A giant tortoise at the Charles Darwin Research Station on the island of Santa Cruz. Giant tortoises may weigh over 500 pounds and may live over 100 years.

or historical, pause. With flamingos stretched out in lugubrious flight over its fur seal grottos; flows of magma orange as a New Mexican sunset percolating from its active volcanos; towering ferns nodding in the wind like trees from the Carboniferous; with its lanky packs of bat-eared feral dogs, some two hundred generations removed from human contact, Galápagos proves unruly to the imagination.

A departing visitor typically recalls being astonished here by the indifference of animals to human superiority. Sea lions continue to doze on the beach as you approach, even as you come to stand within inches of their noses. Their eyes open with no more alarm at your presence than were you parent to their dozing child. Mockingbirds snatch at your hair and worry your shoelaces—you are to them but some odd amalgamation of nesting materials. While this "tameness" is not to be forgotten, and while it is an innocence that profoundly comforts the traveler, Galápagos imparts more important lessons, perhaps, about the chaos of life. A blue-footed booby chick, embraceable in its white down, stands squarely before an ocean breeze, wrestling comically with its new wings, like someone trying to fold a road map in a high wind. An emaciated sea lion pup, rudely shunned by the other adults, waits with resolute cheer for a mother who clearly will never return from the sea. You extend your fingers to the damp, soft rims of orchids here, blooming white on the flanks of dark volcanos.

Santa Cruz, in whose highlands I had gone to hike, lies near the center of the archipelago, some 590 miles west of Ecuador. Almost half of Galápagos's permanent population of 10,000 lives here, on farms, in two small villages, and in the large town of Puerto Ayora. The geography of this island is typical of Galápagos; the character of the vegetation changes, rather sharply, as one gains altitude. Candelabra and prickly pear cactus, dominating in the lowlands, give way to a transitional zone of dry brush. Higher up this scrubland turns to forest, then to heath and open country, where sedges, grasses, and ferns grow. It was while climbing up through these life zones on the slopes of an extinct volcano, hearing wet elephant grass swish against my pants, that I first became aware of my untempered preconception of Galápagos as desolate. And it was here, along a fence line meant to restrain cattle, that I initially encountered the immense and quintessential animal of Galápagos, the giant tortoise. In those first moments it seemed neither a dim nor a clumsy beast. In its saurian aloofness, in the wild shining of its eyes as it ceased its grazing to scrutinize my passage, I beheld a different realm of patience, of edification, than the one I knew. Tortoises hesitate and plunge across the highlands like stunned ursids. The spiritual essence of Galápagos clings to them.

It was also on Santa Cruz, in the streets of Puerto Ayora, that I first sensed the dimensions of something more disturbingly ordinary—the difficulties the people of Galápagos confront today: an erratic economic development that has come with the growth of tourism, and the disaffection of local farmers, fisher-

A small group of flamingos glides in front of a volcanic cone on the island of Floreana, home to some 500 of these spectacular birds.

men, and lobstermen with the distribution of wealth here.

Galápagos seduces the visitor with the complexity of its beauty; but, like any mecca of wonder in the modern era, its beauty, its capacity to heal the traveler from afar, is threatened by the traveler himself, and by the exigencies of modern society. In 1985 a huge, man-caused fire burned nearly a hundred square miles of forest and pampa on southern Isla Isabela. The fire began on the rim of Volcán Santo Tomás and burned for months before an international team of forest fire fighters finally put it out. The press in North America and Europe exaggerated the havoc (penguins, for example, did not flee before the flames nor did flamingos turn gray from a fallout of ash)—and the exaggeration precipitated an indictment. While the cause of the fire remains undetermined, it was widely assumed in the United States and in Europe that it was started, accidently but perhaps on purpose, by residents of the small village of Santo

Tomás. The charred landscape was viewed, by some, as a dark statement of economic frustration, of the village's irritation with officials of Galápagos National Park, who will not allow them to extend their croplands and small-scale ranching operations into the—to them—"unused" interior of the islands; or to cut timber there.

Two extreme views about the future of Galápagos have since emerged. Some scientists, already aware of the extensive damage done in the islands by domestic animals gone wild—there are presently 80,000 feral goats and 5,000 feral pigs on Isla Santiago alone—would like to see the resident human population of Galápagos greatly reduced and most agricultural holdings bought out and incorporated into the park. Many colonists, on the other hand, want to see both tourism and town trade continue to expand, in order to supplement their relatively meager incomes from farming, ranching, fishing, and odd jobs. (Galápagos has no indigenous people with prior land claims. The first colonists arrived in 1832, when Ecuador took possession of the islands.)

But these are the extreme positions. Economic hardship is evident to anyone walking the dirt streets of Galápagos's villages; but, on Isla Santa Cruz at least, the accommodation achieved among colonists, scientists, and national park personnel seems, to one who inquires, of a relatively high order. Considering how recently principles of conservation, let alone land-use planning, have become part of village life in South America, the acquiesence of many farmers to park-service demands for conservation is striking. (In a gesture of reciprocal understanding, park managers recently began planting teak trees on private land, to compensate owners for the saw timber they are not allowed to take from the park.)

Galápagos has two indisputable, interrelated problems: economic develoment (farming, fishing, tourism) without any overall plan; and non-native plants and animals, which continue to change the islands' ecology. The latter situation is dire, but no worse than it's been in recent memory. Programs to eliminate feral goats on some of the smaller islands have been successful, as have efforts to reintroduce tortoises to areas where their populations have been decimated by feral cats, dogs, pigs, and rats. (A new, current worry is that feral dogs may breach a rugged, waterless stretch of lava called the Perry Isthmus on Isabela and begin to prey on the least-disturbed animal populations in the whole archipelago, those on northern Isabela.)

Galápagos National Park incorporates nearly 97 percent of Galápagos, a combined land mass the size of Connecticut.

Male land iguana, reminiscent of a
miniature dragon. This particular species
is endemic to the island of Santa Fé.

(Near-shore waters were recently declared a "marine resource
reserve" by the Ecuadorian government. Tourism and commercial fisheries officials, the park service, and the Ecuadorian navy
are currently working out a management agreement.) The
other 3 percent of the land comprises several hundred square
miles of farmstead, a few small settlements, and three large

villages—Puerto Ayora, a base for tourism and scientific research on Santa Cruz; Puerto Baquerizo Moreno, the islands' administrative center on San Cristóbal; and Puerto Villamil, a farming and ranching community on Isabela. Agriculture in Galápagos has always been marginal, due to a lack of fresh water, poor soils, and periods of drought. Fishing offers an economic alternative, but Galapagean fishermen increasingly are of the view that profit lies with converting their work boats to touring yachts.

Changes in the Galapagean economy are directly related to a sharp rise in tourism. During the 1960s only a few thousand tourists a year visited the archipelago. When the numbers increased in the 1970s, a park committee suggested a limit—12,000 per year, later raised to 25,000. In 1986, for the first time, more than 26,000 came, severely straining hotel and restaurant facilities at Puerto Ayora and more limited facilities at Baquerizo Moreno, the two communities connected to the mainland by air. Officials are now looking for specific answers to three separate questions. How many visitors can the park itself absorb? How many visitors can the park service manage? And how many people can simultaneously be present at a single location in the park before a visitor's sense of the magical remoteness of Galápagos is lost?

Points of legal disembarkation in the park—seabird colonies, cactus forests, saltwater lagoons—are limited, currently to 45; the tour I joined, therefore, took us to the very same spots other visitors see. Occasionally we did encounter another group, but what we saw or heard at nearly every site was so uncommon, so invigorating, that the intrusion of others rarely detracted. We snorkeled amid schools of brilliant sergeant majors and yellow-tailed surgeon fish at a place called the Devil's Crown, off Isla Floreana. At tidal pools on the coast of Santiago, octopuses stared at us askance, and small fish called blennies wriggled past, walking pegleg on their fin tips from pool to pool over the rock. At Isla Española we stepped respectfully around blue-footed boobies nesting obdurately in the trail. At Punta Cormorant we watched a regatta of ghost crabs scurry off up the beach, a high-stepping whir, two hundred or more of them, as if before a stiff breeze.

The genius of the management plan in Galápagos—its success in preserving a feeling of wilderness warrants the word—rests on three principles. The park, first, exercises a high degree of control over where visitors go, with whom, and what they do. No one may travel in the park without a licensed guide and guides can, and sometimes do, send visitors too cavalier

21

about the environment back to the boat; trails are marked and bounds have been established at each visitor site; and touching or feeding the animals, wandering off on one's own, or pocketing so much as a broken seashell are all prohibited. Second, because the boat itself incorporates the services of a hotel, a restaurant, and a souvenir shop, there is no on-shore development aside from the villages. Last, the park works concertedly with the Charles Darwin Research Station, a nonprofit, international scientific program, to manage the islands and monitor their well-being.

As a result of these precautions, few sites appear overused. Occasionally one even has the illusion, because the animals don't flee at your approach, of being among the first to visit.

Galápagos gently, gradually, overpowers. As our small yacht made its long passage between islands at night (to put us at a new island at dawn), I would lie awake trying to remember some moment of the day just past. The very process of calling upon the details of color and sound was a reminder of how provocative the landscape is, to both the senses and the intellect. The sensual images I recalled in vivid bursts; the yellow-white incandesence of an iguana's head; a thick perfume like the odor of frankincense, suspended through a grove of bursera trees. At a sheer headland on Islas Plazas, I watched swallow-tailed gulls rappel a violent draft of air, stall, quivering in the wind, then float slowly backward in the stream of it to land light as a sigh on their cliff nests. One afternoon while we floated on a turquoise lagoon, Pacific green turtles rose continuously to the calm surface to glance at us, the stillness broken only by water tinkling from their carapaces. They drew surprised, audible breath and sank. Behind them a long hillside of leafless palo santo trees shot up, a wall of Chinese calligraphy leaning into an azure sky.

The most enduring image in Galápagos for me, however, was filled with terror rather than beauty. I stood an hour in a storm petrel colony, under heavy gray skies on the east coast of Tower Island. Galápagos and Madeiran petrels, adroit seabirds about the size of a robin but with thin, delicate legs, nested here in cracks and hollows on a flat expanse of barren lava. They were hunted down, even as I watched, by intense, compact, lethal predators—short-eared owls. Wind had scattered the torn fragments of bone and feather like rubbish over the dark plain. Farther back from the sea, boobies and frigatebirds had made nests in the first ranks of low muyuyo shrubs. The risk in these lives was as apparent. Young birds dead of starvation or victims of what ornithologists call sibling murder lay crumpled on the bare ground like abandoned clothing. Detached wings

hung like faded pennants in wickets of *Cordia lutea* bushes, the wreckage of fatal bad landings.

These deaths, one realizes, are all in the flow of natural selection; but the stark terror of it, like the sight of a sea lion's shark-torn flipper, makes the thought fresh and startling. Images of innocent repose and violence are never far apart in Galápagos and the visitor is nowhere spared the contrast. He or she scans the seascape and landscape at the storm petrel colony acutely aware of the light hold the biological has on the slow, brutal upheaval of the geological.

The first humans to visit Galápagos may have been Indians from the South American mainland, who arrived on ocean-going balsa rafts in the eleventh century and probably used the islands only as a base for fishing operations. In 1535 Fray Tomás de Berlanga, Bishop of Panama, sailing far off course, came on the islands by accident and gave them the name that later appeared in Abraham Ortelius's atlas of 1570—*Insulae de los Galápagos*. (The cleft fore-edge of a lowland tortoise's carapace resembles the sharply rising pommel of a sixteenth-century Spanish saddle, the old Spanish for which was *galopego*.) English buccaneers began using the islands as a raiding base late in the seventeenth century. Struck by the contrariness of local winds, they renamed the place *las encantadas*, the enchanted ones.

Early in the nineteenth century whalers began visiting Galápagos regularly. They came to hunt sperm whales west of Isabela but found they were also able to careen their boats easily on the beaches for repairs and to provision them quickly with live tortoises, a source of fresh meat. The whalers turned pigs and goats loose on most of the islands, food for anyone who came up shipwrecked, but, too, animals easy to hunt down on a return visit. They barreled fresh water in the odd year when it was readily available. They idly beat thousands of marine iguanas and Galápagos doves to death with sticks, marveling at how the animals "do not get out of our way." And they buried their dead among the stones.

The legacy of those frontier days of whaling (and later of sealing) is still evident in Galápagos. Only 15,000 of an original population of perhaps 200,000 tortoises remain; four of fifteen subspecies are extinct and another is on the verge of extinction. The fur seal population, almost hunted out, is making a slow recovery; and black rats (from the ships) long ago eliminated at least one species of rice rat, the lone native mammals on the islands, aside from bats. Foraging goats have radically altered the structure of some of the island's plant communities.

In addition to the whalers and sealers, three other groups, historically, had an impact on the biology of Galápagos. During World War II, American soldiers stationed on Baltra shot virtually all the larger animals there, and scientists, during the late nineteenth and early twentieth centuries, collected extensively for zoos and museums. The most deleterious effects, however, were caused by colonists.

The history of colonization in Galápagos is marked to an unusual degree by violence and periods of wretched, bare subsistence. The early settlements, founded on the hope of trading agricultural products to the mainland, all failed. In due course, each was turned into a penal colony by the Ecuadorian government. Attempts to raise sugarcane, coffee, citrus fruits, melons, and sweet potatoes, and small-scale efforts to export sulfur, seal hides, and tortoise oil, or to make stock-ranching profitable, were all schemes that didn't take sufficiently into account

Bleached coral heads at Urvina Bay on Isabela, stranded when the surrounding sea floor was uplifted by up to 20 feet in 1954, are part of the changing geology of the Galápagos. Terrestrial vegetation is gradually starting to take over this parched seascape.

The Galapagos dove, seen here on Santa Fé, is unique to the islands. Its tameness and lack of fear led to its being slaughtered by the hundreds for sport and food by early human visitors.

the thinness of the volcanic soils, the undependable climate, or the vicissitudes of a trade-based economy.

Along with the farmers came resident fishermen who fared somewhat better. Utopian daydreamers, adventurers, and eccentrics followed, many of them poorly informed about the islands' climate, the extent of its arable lands, even their sovereign status. This pattern, in fact, carried far into the twentieth century.

The first scientific collectors in the islands, an expedition under the French, arrived in 1790. The next, under Captain Fitz-Roy in HMS *Beagle* in 1835, fixed the archipelago indelibly in the minds of all who read the subsequent reports of the ship's naturalist, Charles Darwin. In 1905–06 the California Academy of Sciences conducted the last major effort to collect in the islands, with an apparent excess of zeal—its leader killed the only tortoise ever recorded on Isla Fernandina.

The days when scientists trapped for zoos and collected indiscriminately are gone; settlers, however, still turn domestic animals loose to prey upon, and compete with, native animals, and residents still shoot Galápagos hawks as predators and occasionally poach tortoise meat. Colonists have also introduced nearly 250 exotic plants to the islands, some of which, in combination with the grazing of feral horses, goats, cattle, and donkeys, threaten several endemic plants with extinction. Scientists, too, occasionally contribute to alterations in the islands' plant communities by bringing food and equipment ashore that harbor seeds or insects from the mainland, or from one of the other islands.

Anxiety about the islands' natural communities stems from scientific knowledge that each island's flora and fauna are unique. Remarkably, this remains essentially true today, despite plant introductions, damage by feral animals, and the loss of some native plant and animal populations. Researchers, in other words, can still find in Galápagos an evolutionary puzzle with relatively few pieces missing.

A desire to preserve a virtually undisturbed environment in the islands seems obsessive and unrealistic to some local villagers and farmers. Their pressing concerns are for food, a stable source of fresh water, and such things as raw building materials and supplementary income. (One encounters this basic difference in point of view, of course, with growing frequency in many countries now, around the game parks of East Africa, for example, or in the rain forests of Guatemala.) In Galápagos, as elsewhere, things of the mind, including the intellectual ramifications of evolutionary theory, and things of the spirit, like the feeling one gets from a Queen Anne's lace of stars in the moonless Galapagean sky, struggle toward accommodation with an elementary desire for material comfort. In Galápagos, however, the measure of accommodation is slightly different. Things of the mind and spirit exert more influence here because so many regard this archipelago as preeminently a terrain of the mind and the spirit, a locus of biological thought and psychological rejuvenation. It represents the legacy of Charles Darwin, and the heritage of devotion to this thought.

The sheer strength alone of Darwin's insight into the arrangement of biological life gently urges a visitor to be more than usually observant here, to notice, say, that while the thirteen Galapagean finches are all roughly the same hue, that it is possible to separate them according to marked differences in the shapes of their bills and feeding habits. The eye catches similar nuances elsewhere—minor differences also separate eleven species of tortoise and fourteen species of *Scalesia* tree.

31

This close variety is tantalizing. Invariably, one begins to wonder why these related species look so much alike—and an encounter with adaptive radiation, with what Darwin called "descent with modification," becomes inevitable.

A vague intellectual current meanders continually through Galápagos, an ever-present musing one senses among a certain steady stream of visitors, if but faintly. Evolution, an elegantly simple perception, is clarified by exceedingly complex speculation; Darwin's heroic attempt to understand evolutionary change forms part of the atmospheric pressure in Galápagos. And the idea that an elucidation of natural selection or genetic drift, mechanisms by which evolution might operate, could contribute to more than just a clearer understanding of the universe, that it might make humanity's place in it plainer, is never far off.

One has no need, of course, to know how natural selection might have directed their destinies to appreciate unadorned variety among Darwin's finches. The Galápagos penguin is no less startling, the turquoise eyes of the cormorant no less riveting, for not knowing precisely how each might have evolved since it arrived. Nor is a visitor required to brood over the economic fate of farmers and villagers in Galápagos, while staring down into the wondrous blowhole of a dolphin riding the bow wave of a tour boat. But at the close of the twentieth century, not to turn to the complexities of evolution in a real place, to the metaphorical richness and utility of Darwin's thought, or to turn away from the economic aspirations of a local people, seems to risk much. Our knowledge of life is slim. The undisturbed landscapes are rapidly dwindling. And no plan has yet emerged for a kind of wealth that will satisfy all people.

As I sailed between the islands—at dawn from the sea they look like the heads of crows emerging from the ocean—I dwelled on the anomalies. Subsistence hunters pursue feral cattle high up on the Sierra Negra with dogs and snares, the same cattle that are pursued by packs of resident feral dogs. What meat they get they sell in Puerto Villamil for $.13 a pound. From their mountain redoubt they watch the tour boats far below, steaming east along the coastal margin. The park's wardens work 364 days a year for $1,650, part of it on 20-day patrols in the arid, rugged interior, hunting down feral dogs and goats to purify the park. A young farmer, proud of his shrewdness, says he will grow a diversity of condiment crops on his small holding and so be in a strong and exclusive position to supply new restaurants, which are sure to come to Puerto Ayora. I remember an afternoon sitting at the Darwin Research

Station, reading formal descriptions of nearly a hundred scientific projects underway in the islands. What a concise presentation of the inexhaustible range of human inquiry, I thought, what invigorating evidence of the desire to understand.

The evening before I departed I stood on the rim of a lagoon on Isla Rábida. Flamingos rode on its dark surface like pink swans, apparently asleep. Small, curved feathers, shed from their breasts, drifted away from them over the water on a light breeze. I did not move for an hour. It was a moment of such peace every troubled thread in a human spirit might have uncoiled and sorted itself into graceful order. Other flamingos

A Galápagos penguin preparing to enter the waters of Elizabeth Bay, off the island of Isabela. These penguins are the only ones known to nest north of the equator.

OVERLEAF:
Marine iguanas draped over shoreline rocks on the island of Fernandina.

33

stood in the shallows with diffident elegance in the falling light, not feeding but only staring off toward the ocean. They seemed a kind of animal I had never quite seen before.

II

I left for Quito with regrets. I had eaten the flesh of blue lobster and bacalao from Galápagos waters and enjoyed prolonged moments of intimacy with the place; but I had not, as I had hoped, the days to climb Volcán Alcedo, nor had I seen a shark or a violent thunderstorm. But I knew that I would be back. It was not the ethereal beauty of the flamingos, solely, or the dazzling appearance underwater of a school of blue-eyed damselfish that now pulled at me. It was the fastness of the archipelago, the fullness of its life; and the juxtaposition of violent death that signaled that more than scenery was here.

On the way to the hotel, the cab driver spoke about Galápagos with resignation and yearning. A number of Ecuadorians think of Galápagos the way Americans once dreamed of the West, a place where one might start life over, fresh. I told him about a young couple who had just opened a small restaurant in the hills above Puerto Ayora. I had had coffee there after a long hike. I sat by myself on the veranda, watching sunlight filter through the forest. Far in the distance I could see the pale ocean. I could hear bird song, which sharpened an irrational feeling of allegiance, of fierce camaraderie, with the light, the wild tortoises I had seen that afternoon, the vermilion flycatchers that had followed me.

As we threaded our way through heavy traffic and billowing diesel exhaust from the municipal buses, the driver asked what sorts of birds I had seen. I told him. The litany made him gesture at the traffic, the different makes of vehicle pinning us in, and led him to smile ruefully.

"¿Por que quieres ir a la Galápagos?" I asked. Why do you wish to go to Galápagos? For work? To buy a farm?

"La paz," he said, turning to look at me, his thin, sharp face full of fervent belief. The peace.

Ah, Galápagos is not peaceful I thought. It is full of the wild conflict that defines life. The groaning of the earth beneath fumaroles on Fernandina. Owl-dashed petrels. But what I reflected on wasn't what he meant at all. He meant a reprieve. Retreat. I thought to tell him, as I put the fare in his hand, of the flamingos on Rábida. People in Frankfurt and San Francisco, in

Quito and Puerto Ayora and Geneva, I wanted to say, are working to ensure that this will remain possible, a place out there in the ocean where men and women might gather themselves again. It would take wisdom and courtesy to effect, a certain understanding among those who wish fewer people would come and those who want to see more. An understanding that what is beautiful and mysterious belongs to no one, is in fact a gift.

But these were my own feelings, too presuming. What came out of me, as I nodded gratitude for a desultory conversation in an unfamiliar city, was *Hallar la paz, esto muy juicioso . . .* To go there to find peace, that is very wise.

I turned to see my bags gone from the sidewalk, the doorman smiling, holding the door patiently, cordiality in the sweep of his gloved hand.

The vermilion flycatcher is the most colorful of the Galápagos land birds. It feeds on small insects that it catches during short flights from its moss-covered perch in the highlands, here on Santa Cruz.

Santa Cruz

ISLAND OF MANY FACES

A lush forest of *Scalesia* trees surrounds a pit crater and gracefully cloaks an old volcanic cone in the distance. *Scalesia,* native to the Galápagos and prominent in the highlands of Santa Cruz, are the majestic arboreal relatives of sunflowers and daisies, attaining heights of up to 60 feet.

Santa Cruz, the most frequently visited island in the archipelago, is often described as the point of embarkation for any Galápagos journey. Centrally located, it is only a short ferry ride away from the Baltra airstrip, the most common means of entry to the islands. Here, in the town of Puerto Ayora, travelers can charter small boats to farther-flung Galápagos destinations, and here, too, one mile to the east on the coast of Academy Bay, one may experience a positive result of human habitation—the Charles Darwin Research Station, a haven of scientific inquiry and information and a breeding spot for the famed giant tortoise.

Santa Cruz is truly an island of diversity, from its precarious balance of settlement and conservation to its wildly differing landscape, vegetation, and animal life. Reaching almost 3,000 feet above sea level, Santa Cruz offers visible, dramatic changes in its flora and fauna from one area to another. At the sea's edge is a tangled fringe of mangroves and green, salt-tolerant plants. The area just inland from this littoral "zone" is arid forest, dominated by palo santo trees (the name *palo santo* is Spanish for "holy stick," which refers to this normally leafless (to conserve water), silver-barked plant's characteristic of coming into flower around Christmastime—the start of the rainy season) and the *Opuntia,* or prickly pear cactus. Lava lizards, mockingbirds, and ground finches are the most obvious denizens of this region. Farther inland and upward, the vegetation becomes denser and more varied, slowly becoming transformed into an almost magical, mist-shrouded region of tall trees, covered with mosses and liverworts. This area, originally marked by the native evergreen *Scalesia,* was one of the earliest regions to become cultivated, and consequently much of the zone has given way to pastures and small plantations. Tropical, yet temperate, these beautiful forests are home to the vermilion flycatcher and many species of tree finch. Beyond lies the *Miconia* (a dense bush endemic to two of the islands) zone, above which, instead of shrubs or trees, looms a prehistoric-looking jungle of ferns, sedges, and grasses, wrapped in fog.

The variety found on Santa Cruz is also geological. In terms of geology, Santa Cruz is relatively old. The "younger" parts of the island are marked by eroded volcanic cones called "cerros" (the most famous being Cerro Crocker). Other features include spatter cones (such as Puntudo), formed by the "spattering" of molten material from an active volcano, and pit craters, small calderas, of which the Gemelos (or "twins") are the most notable.

Tortuga Bay, one of the most breath-taking of Galápagos beaches, is reached by a three-and-a-half-mile hike from the town of Puerto Ayora. On the right of the photograph, the tangled aerial roots of red mangroves are visible, while watchful brown pelicans perch in a white mangrove tree on the left.

Giant tortoises wallow in a temporary pastureland pool formed during the rainy season. Santa Cruz is the location of the most accessible, although not the largest giant tortoise habitat in the archipelago, and a reserve area has been set up on the south side of the island. On this sole cultivated area of the Galápagos, these uncultivated beasts can often be seen slipping under farmers' barbed-wire fences and into their cattle-grazing pastures.

Lichen-covered palo santo trees, prickly pear, and stately candelabra cacti dominate the arid zone.

The transition-zone forest fuses elements of the upper wet zone and the lower dry regions into a wonderfully strange microclimate. Here, a prickly pear cactus provides support for a passionflower vine.

42

A small temporary stream in the pampa, or fern-sedge zone, an eerie, damp moorland often shrouded in mist.

The highest point on the island of Santa Cruz, Cerro Crocker, seen from the crater of the Puntudo spatter cone. An introduced agave or century plant grows alongside huge native tree ferns called *Cyathea,* which often have parasol-like fronds six feet or more in length. Because of the island's relative age, the vegetation in this area is quite thick and has nearly overgrown the crater.

Fog-soaked highland greenery at the border of the fern-sedge zone and the shrubby belt of the *Miconia* zone. The *Miconia* zone exists only on Santa Cruz and on the island of San Cristóbal.

Delicate lichen carpets the way leading to the characteristic tall sides of Puntudo.

Genovesa

A TOWER OF SEABIRDS

A masked booby with its chick surveys Darwin Bay from atop the steep cliffs known as Prince Phillip's Steps, named after a royal conservationist.

OVERLEAF:
Darwin Bay, named for but never actually visited by Charles Darwin, was created by the collapse of layers of volcanic lava into a caldera. Its intensely blue waters are as much as 600 feet deep. The encircling cliffs bear the traces and streaked patterns of successive lava flows and contain many crevices and fissures. Red-billed tropicbirds can be seen nesting in the crevices and frequently perform dramatic flight stunts during the afternoon hours. Sea lions and fur seals are often found in the shaded caves and on the large flat rocks at the water's edge.

A distant sail away from the central islands, at the northeastern edge of the archipelago, lies Genovesa. One of the most pristine of the Galápagos group, it is the remote refuge of many thousands of oceanic birds. Genovesa, as a result of its isolation, remains an undisturbed nesting ground for these birds, who fish in its rich waters, and lacks introduced as well as native land animals and reptiles—the only reptile, in fact, is a small subspecies of marine iguana.

The island itself is the summit of a huge inactive undersea volcano, which protrudes above the water a scant 250 feet. The main vent of the volcano, a large circular caldera, or collapse crater, with a saltwater lake some 200 feet deep on its floor, depresses the center of the island, while the southern side of Genovesa, the site of a partially eroded crater, is scooped out to form Darwin Bay. At sea level, cliff-bound Darwin Bay is the most accessible of the calderas. Boats anchoring in the bay will usually become perches for red-footed boobies in search of food, and a frigatebird or two may easily take up residence in the upper riggings.

Visitors stepping onto land find themselves instantly in the midst of vast seabird colonies. Genovesa is home to what is probably the largest collection of red-footed boobies (up to 140,000 pairs), who nest in the gray palo santo trees dotting the cliffs. Overhead, criss-crossing the sky, are gleaming white swallow-tailed gulls, silently gliding frigatebirds, and the hosts of red-billed tropicbirds and black-and-white Audubon shearwaters that occupy the deep openings in the mountainous lava formations. The southeastern cliffs are alive with one of island's largest colonies of wedge-rumped petrals (up to 200,000 pairs), tiny, nocturnal birds that share the small point of land with their daylight-loving relatives, the delicate band-rumped petrals. Toward the interior of the island, which is covered with stocky, low-growing prickly pear and is generally arid, four species of Darwin's finches can be found, and the Galápagos dove can be seen bobbing along under bushes and over the lava, looking for seeds.

Genovesa's central caldera contains jade and turquoise brackish waters rimmed with salt-tolerant plant life. Elsewhere, bare palo santo trees, often holding the nests of red-footed boobies, dot the landscape.

Short-eared owl, the only predatory bird found on Genovesa, where it feeds chiefly in the storm-petrel colonies. On this island, the owl is active during the day, but on islands where competitors are found—the hawk and the barn owl—it is nocturnal.

An immature red-footed booby studies the sea's surface in search of potential prey. This bird is often encountered on the ocean because it feeds in deep offshore waters.

Swallow-tailed gulls take to the air from the seaside cliffs where they roost in loose colonies that may number in the hundreds or thousands of birds. With its brightly patterned head distinguished by huge black eyes ringed in a striking orange and its white forked tail, the gull is one of the most eye-catching species to see on the wing.

The red-footed booby is most easily identified by its blue beak and pink face, since the red feet after which it takes its name are often hidden while the bird is perched or in flight, and the adult plumage may be either brown or black-and-white like that of a masked booby. Young red-footed boobies do not develop the bright facial coloration until they reach adulthood.

The tidal lagoon behind the small beach at Darwin Bay is home to many tiny blennies and fiddler crabs. The lagoon is frequently visited by yellow-crowned night herons in search of small fish and crabs. A plethora of seabird colonies, including those of swallow-tailed gulls, redfooted and masked boobies, and the great frigatebird, surrounds the lagoon. Here, a swallow-tailed gull appears almost irridescent in the dusky feeding hours.

A male great frigatebird displays his red pouch in the hope of attracting a female flying above. This colorful display is accompanied by ululating calls and is one of the most spectacular sights of the Galápagos. At right, the bird's pouch is stretched, it seems, almost to the point of bursting. The pouch is kept inflated for long periods of time and will remain so even during flight. Once frigatebirds nest, they construct flimsy nesting platforms in the low saltbushes or in palo santo trees.

A frigatebird cruises over a beach—inviting comparisons to the prehistoric pterodactyl—perhaps in search of nesting material, which it will most likely steal from a hapless booby or even from its own species. Roving frigatebirds are often seen stealing twigs, eggs, or small young from the nests of other seabirds. They are known as man-of-war birds because of their piratic habits.

A male great frigatebird with his pouch
partly inflated soars effortlessly above
Darwin Bay at sunset. Frigatebirds are
among the world's most agile fliers,
with a wingspan to weight ratio greater
than that of any other species—eight
feet in relation to two or three pounds
for adult birds.

Floreana
HOME OF THE FLAMINGOS

Flamingos preen in a shallow lagoon at Punta Cormorant on Floreana beneath the rise of a volcanic tuff cone dusted with feathery, leafless palo santo trees.

The island of Floreana rests south of Santa Cruz, rising and falling in a proliferation of volcanic cones, which are often gentled by a thin mantle of palo santo forest. The sterner, western part of the island consists of bare lava flows and a striking black sand beach. At the northeastern corner, however, one finds Punta Cormorant, whose lagoon frequently harbors the elegant flamingo as well as several other species of birds that feed in the still, clouded waters.

Only some five hundred of the proud pink flamingos inhabit the entire Galápagos Islands, spread out over several lagoons and ponds. As conditions dictate, they move from one lagoon to another, so that they are rarely seen in groups of more than a few dozen at a time. Despite their small numbers, flamingos are social breeders and nest together following an elaborate courtship display during which the birds perform in choreographed "parades" back and forth with their necks stretched up and feathers fluffed.

Floreana has the most interesting human history of the settled islands, (which encompass Santa Cruz, Isabela, Floreana, and San Cristóbal), in addition to being a place of great natural beauty. The first colonist of the Galápagos, an Irishman named Patrick Watkins, is thought to have been stranded on Floreana in 1807 and subsisted by selling food supplies to visiting whaling ships. In 1832 the Galápagos were officially claimed by Ecuador and "Charles" Island was renamed Floreana, after the first president of Ecuador. A strange bit of twentieth-century lore involves a somewhat crazed German philosopher, Friedrich Ritter, and his mistress; a couple from Berlin, Heinz and Margaret Wittmer; and the self-styled "Empress of the Galápagos," Baroness Eloisa von Wagner Bosquet from Austria, and her two lovers. During the 1930s these were the only inhabitants of Floreana, and there was little friendship among the three groups. Within a few years, Ritter had died mysteriously of "food poisoning," the baroness and a lover had disappeared, and the second lover died trying to get away to another island. To this day there is no clear account of what happened, although three books (most notably *The Galápagos Affair* by John Treherne) and several articles have been written about the "Floreana story." Margaret Wittmer continues to live with her family on Floreana, where she runs a small café.

A regal group of Galápagos greater flamingos feeds quietly in the salty lagoon at Punta Cormorant. Flamingos filter the rich, brackish waters with their long bills for small insects and shrimp. The chemicals produced by the food supply is responsible for the characteristic pink color of these birds.

Greater flamingos in flight. The black wing feathers are visible only when these magnificent birds take flight.

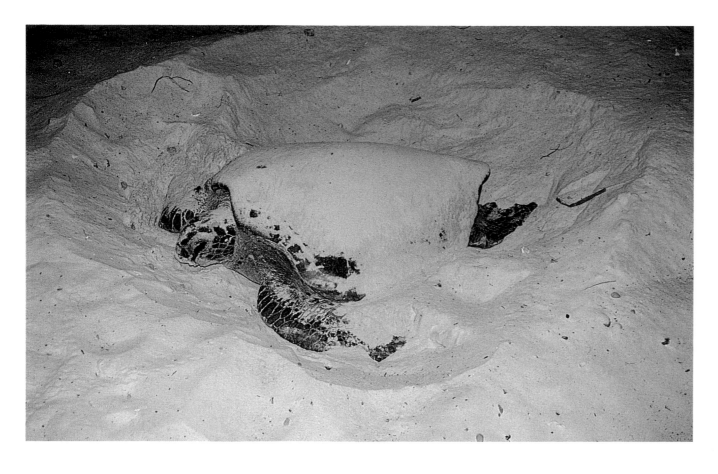

A Pacific green sea turtle comes on shore at night to lay her eggs: after digging a nest, she deposits the eggs and then covers the nest depression before returning to the water. For much of the year these shy creatures are seen only when they come to the surface of the water to draw breath. Late in the year, however, the quiet lagoons of the Galápagos, like those found in abundance on Floreana, become the favorite mating areas for this species of turtle.

A young brown pelican on the north beach at Punta Cormorant. The pelican, widespread in the Galápagos, uses its long, pouched bill to retrieve fish after plunging gracelessly into the sea with splashy, shallow dives.

The cocoa-brown beach at Punta Cormorant gets its color from eroded fragments of the surrounding volcanic cones. The shore is composed primarily of terrestrial minerals and other materials due to its location sheltering it from the prevailing winds and ocean currents.

Evening light on the flamingo lagoon
at Punta Cormorant. The hairy-leafed
Scalesia villosa bushes in the fore-
ground of the photograph are endemic to this part of Floreana and are
found nowhere else in the world.

OPPOSITE:
Shades of brown dominate the Floreana landscape at Punta Cormorant,
however, its compelling color is the result not of unique Galapagean features
but of vegetation that has been rav-
aged by feral goats.

OVERLEAF:
The drying lagoon, giving off a silvery-
pink shimmer. The feeding lagoon frequently dries up in areas, revealing the
muddy pinkish ooze that supplies the
flamingos with food. Fluctuating lagoon
levels cause the birds to move from
one lagoon to another.

View from the larger volcanic cone over the beaches and lagoon at Punta Cormorant. The small offshore island, Devil's Crown, is an eroded cone and an excellent snorkeling site. Unlike the brown beach at the left of the photograph, the beach at right faces the winds and the force of ocean waves and is thus composed of fine white shell and coral sand. Stingrays are commonly seen swimming a few feet off this beautiful beach.

Volcán Alcedo, Isabela
LAND OF THE GIANT TORTOISES

Two giant tortoises pause on the rim of Volcán Alcedo. A giant tortoise may weigh 550 pounds, and in 1845 Charles Darwin described a tortoise as requiring six to eight men to move it. Today, about 5,000 of these impressive creatures are estimated to live on Alcedo and its flanks.

To reach the top of Volcán Alcedo is to enter the heart of the Galápagos giant tortoise "empire." Swelling from the middle of the volcanic chain that stretches across the island of Isabela, Alcedo, with its large caldera and long, narrow rim, supports the largest population of these mammoth tortoises in the archipelago. A natural wonder in its own right, Alcedo's rim—unique among visitor sites in the islands in that overnight camping is permitted here—affords views of spectacular sunrises and sunsets. An impressive sight just inside the southern edge of the rim is the volcano's fumarole, with its plume of white steam rising several hundred feet above the roaring vent. The fumarole is the only volcanic activity here, since Volcán Alcedo has not erupted in recent years. The volcano was still active seismically, however, as late as 1954, when a section of its coastline at Urvina Bay was uplifted by several feet, stranding a thriving coral reef community.

Alcedo's rim crowns the volcano's 3,500-foot slopes. Along its twenty-mile expanse runs a network of trails etched by lumbering tortoises as they move to ever-wetter areas with the changing seasons, in search of cooling moisture and vegetation for food. During the "dry" garúa (fog) season, the tortoises cluster along the lusher southeastern part of the rim, which is then bathed in a fine mist, nourishing the orchids, ferns, mosses, and lichens clinging to the trees and bushes. Underneath the trees, small pools form as a result of water collecting on the epiphytes and falling to the ground below, and these become favorite resting places for tortoises. During the warm, rainy season, the animals scatter over the rim and onto the caldera floor, where temporary pools provide wallowing areas. In the early summer months, nesting females trek down to drier, lower elevations to dig egg-laying cavities.

The giant tortoises of Alcedo make up one of the five subspecies that live on each of Isabela's five main volcanos. The rubble-like aa (Hawaiian for "hurt") lava flows found between the volcanos are almost impassable and have formed barriers to tortoise movement, allowing each population to exist and evolve independently. The Alcedo group features the dome-shaped carapaces typical of tortoises found on the heavily vegetated islands, in contrast to those from the lower, more desert-like islands, which have saddle-shaped shells and are smaller. Variation between subspecies of tortoises in different parts of the archipelago was one of the factors that prompted Charles Darwin to consider the "origin of species."

Alcedo's rim hosts a variety of bird life, many species of which have developed a symbiotic or at least a fortunate relationship with the tortoises. A finch or a mockingbird will pick insects off the larger animal for food, cleaning the tortoise in the process. The Galápagos hawk and the vermilion flycatcher find the back of the giant tortoise an excellent observation post from which to sight their prey. Below, an immature hawk has a convenient lookout.

A young Galápagos hawk sits in a tree on the volcano's rim. Galápagos hawks are extremely inquisitive birds and will often follow visitors as they hike along the volcano. This fearlessness prompted Darwin to note that he was able to push an unresisting hawk out of a tree branch with the muzzle of a gun.

Two views together provide a panorama of Alcedo's approximately 4-mile-wide caldera. To the right (and north) is Devil's Elbow, where the rim trail narrows to only a few feet. To the north, the climate becomes drier and the vegetation becomes sparser. To the left, lushly forested areas of trees and ferns can be seen.

OVERLEAF:
Heavy cloud just clears the rim above Alcedo's fumarole, or steam vent. Due to the heavy rainfall, this area is tropically rich and covered in ferns, mosses, orchids, and *Peperomia*.

OPPOSITE AND TOP:
A Galápagos hawk in flight shows its
barred tail feathers.

A male vermilion flycatcher decorates
a *Tournefortia* bush on the rim. These
birds are found on many of the Galápagos islands in humid highland areas.

A lone giant tortoise wanders in a small clearing on Alcedo's rim.

Giant tortoises rest in a temporary pool on the floor of Alcedo's caldera. The pools, accumulations of rainwater or "dew" from the dense fog known as the *garúa*, are quickly churned into mud puddles by the animals who use them to keep cool.

Alcedo offers stark contrasts in life and death: giant tortoises mate among tree ferns (left); while the bleached carapace of a deceased tortoise (right), here still retaining a few of its original scales, is a vivid presence amid the foliage.

ABOVE:
A tortoise makes its way to its burrow. Continuous tortoise activity over the years has bared the ground and created a system of surprisingly well-developed trails along the volcano's rim.

OPPOSITE:
Small young giant tortoises graze at the base of an epiphyte-laden tree on Alcedo's rim. The tortoises are vegetarian. The clearing looks out over the volcano's rim to the sea, where James Bay, Santiago, is visible in the distance.

OVERLEAF:
View from Alcedo's rim southeast across a velvet-green forest to the sea 3,500 feet below.

Volcán Chico, Isabela
THE YOUNGEST VOLCANO

Glowing yellow sulfur deposits cover part of the Volcán Chico eruption area, located on the edge of an older important caldera—that of Sierra Negra.

In November 1979, a mile-and-a-half-long fissure opened on the northeastern rim of Isabela's Volcán Sierra Negra. Lava began to pour out from several vents, forming the area now known as Volcán Chico, or "little volcano," and snaked down toward the sea at Elizabeth Bay. Today, clouds of volcanic gases and steam billowing from the eruption site are enduring evidence of this youthful geological outburst. As a result of the hydrothermal activity, large quantities of minerals are dissolved by the steam and carried to surface where they are splattered. Similar activity in many parts of the world has been responsible for creating valuable mineral deposits, and the sulfur accumulations on the western side of Sierra Negra have been mined for short periods of time, but in this often forbidding terrain, without success.

The 1979 eruption was only the most recent in a series of volcanic explosions that have occurred in the Sierra Negra area. The last prior eruption took place in April 1963 and continued for a month, smothering the volcano's eastern flanks. Sierra Negra is considered the oldest of Isabela's six volcanos, as its caldera, or crater, is wide and relatively shallow. Caldera formation, the result of the collapse of the central part of a volcano into the magma chamber that fed the surface eruptions, can occur over and over again, gradually widening the crater and reducing the height of the volcano. The caldera floor is frequently covered by subsequent lava flows, and eruptions can continue to break out along weak zones, such as at Volcán Chico.

A compelling sight, the raw geology of Volcán Chico is reached by a combination of road and hiking trail from the small village of Puerto Villamil on the southern coast of Isabela. Once at the rim of the Sierra Negra caldera, the road (built in part in 1985 to aid in fighting a fire that devastated over 80 square miles of the volcano's southern slopes) gives way to a path, increasingly marked with volcanic debris. Fine, glassy slivers of black lava, frozen into strands from molten material flung high into the air before cooling and falling back to earth, become eerily beautiful signs that one is approaching a rare encounter with primitive forces.

Three views of the caldera of Sierra Negra, the largest of the calderas in the Galápagos at 4½ by 6¼ miles across. The southern part of the rim is often blanketed by the heavy mist called the *garúa*, while the drier northern rim usually basks under clear skies.

The rugged landscape of Volcán Chico bears witness to its recent volcanic activity. The steep-sided cone in the distance was the site of a fountain of molten lava and the source of several lava flows in the area.

Pioneering plant species struggle to gain a foothold in the harsh environment surrounding Volcán Chico and can be found reaching out from the older lavas and from ash and cinder deposits.

Steam continues to vent from fuma-roles at Volcán Chico. Water percolat-ing through the hot rocks below is turned into steam, which rises back up to the surface. The steam provides enough moisture to support fern growth inside the vents. Many of the vapors are sulfurous, creating deposits of crys-tals, which collect on the sides of the spatter cone.

View of lava-encrusted landscape, evidence of ancient fast-flowing volcanic streams.

Punta Vicente Roca, Isabela PARADISE POINT

Overview of the inner and outer coves at Punta Vicente Roca. The secluded inner cove is connected to the sea by subterranean passageways through the tuff cone (composed of hardened layers of volcanic ash) at the base of the cliffs of Volcán Ecuador. The sheltered cove harbors a small colony of sea lions and a blue-footed booby colony.

At the mouth of the "sea horse's head" that forms northern Isabela, the small promontory known as Punta Vicente Roca presides over a pair of jewel-like coves. The coves lie on either side of the eroded remains of a tuff, or volcanic ash cone, which make up the point. Facing the ocean is a bay, shielded from the open swells. The bay is a popular anchorage for boats, from which visitors may transfer to dinghies and ride around the surrounding cliffs—actually the interior walls of a fallen volcano—and perhaps into the partly flooded cave. The area is also a rewarding scuba-diving site, its abundant ocean life the product of cool, nutrient-rich waters upwelling off the volcano's steep submarine slopes. On the other side of the point is a secluded cove, accessible from the sea only through water-filled subterranean passages. Sea lions travel through these passageways and gather on the protected beaches of the hidden waters. Large numbers of blue-footed and masked boobies inhabit the point and the sheer cliffs, and flightless cormorants can be seen along the shoreline.

Punta Vicente Roca itself rests on the southwestern edge of Volcán Ecuador. Rising some 2,600 feet, Isabela's sixth volcano is really half a volcano—the other half having slid into the ocean eons ago. Travelers rounding Cape Berkeley by boat, heading out from the central islands, are treated to the magnificent cutaway view of the volcano and its caldera.

Through a telephotographic lens, sea lions hauled up on the beach, or swimming and gamboling along with bathing blue-footed boobies, can be observed.

Sheer cliffs of the outer wall of the tuff cone at Punta Vicente Roca provide ledges for nesting noddy terns and resting spots for the point's enormous colony of blue-footed boobies.

Blue-footed boobies pepper the sky in front of the steep cliffs of Volcán Ecuador.

ABOVE:
A pair of blue-footed boobies at the colonial nesting grounds. The female (on the right) is larger than the male and has a dark iris, which gives it the appearance of having a larger pupil than the male. The female's call is a loud honking, while the male makes a shrill whistle.

OPPOSITE:
Masked boobies prefer to nest on the steeper slopes. The distinctively marked masked booby is the largest of the boobies.

OVERLEAF:
Two photographs make up a panoramic view of Volcán Ecuador's cutaway caldera. Half of the volcano has dropped over time into the ocean to the west, leaving a dramatic cross section and the volcano's caldera. A cascade of lava has filled much of the caldera floor, and a second tuff cone is visible in the distance on the other side of the caldera. The equator runs just north of the tuff cone.

The dark cliffs of Volcán Ecuador loom
above the pale tuffs of the eroded
cone at Punta Vicente Roca.

View along the rim of the tuff cone
shrouded in thin clouds.

Santiago

Puerto Egas,

VOLCANIC BEACH

Green algae coats a tuffstone rock on the beach, giving it a downy finish. The tidepools of this shoreline area are filled with octopi, four-eyed blennies, and hermit crabs, among many other forms of marine life.

OVERLEAF:
Hardened volcanic ash takes on intricate, organ-like contours on the beach at Puerto Egas.

Named after Hector Egas, the owner of an ill-fated salt-mining company during the 1960s, Puerto Egas carves out a corner of James Bay, on the western end of the lava-coated island of Santiago. Like many commercial ventures in the Galápagos, this attempt (and its predecessor in the 1920s) to extract a profitable mineral from the salt-lake crater immediately beyond the shiny volcanic fields that make up the coast at Puerto Egas was doomed to failure. Today, a few roads and the remains of abandoned buildings serve as reminders of these abortive efforts.

Most visitors to this area of James Bay come to see the shoreline south of Puerto Egas, with its striated yellow, brown, and black cliffs of tuffstone, or hardened volcanic ash, which has also been eroded, molded, and polished by the sea into coves and elaborately patterned rocky beaches. Hikers on the coastal trail may be privileged to spot whales or dolphins cruising by offshore or a feeding frenzy of hundreds of boobies or pelicans attacking a school of fish. At the end of the trail is a magnificent lava-walled grotto whose shady crevices shelter a small group of fur seals.

Perhaps the single dominant feature of the Puerto Egas/James Bay region is a volcanic cone called Sugarloaf, which rises almost 1,300 feet. Formed as the result of the explosive interaction of hot molten rock and cool seawater, this tuff cone and its 700-foot neighbor to the south produced the sandy layers of volcanic ash visible in the nearby cliffs. To the north and east is a large lava flow (noted by Charles Darwin in his journals in 1835), in which fragments of ceramic pots stashed by buccaneers and dated 1684 were later found—establishing an age bracket for this volcanic activity.

The landscape surrounding James Bay is harsh, covered primarily by a sparse forest of palo santo trees, which is threatened by the large population of feral goats on the island who have consumed all but the most unpalatable and heavily armored of native vegetation. The land is consequently turning into an open savannah, and a herd of goats moving across the island calls to mind wildlife on the plains of East Africa. The National Parks Department hopes to remove most of the goats, but without adequate funds for doing so on this relatively large island, temporary measures, such as fencing off some areas of native plant life, must suffice. Despite this destruction of vegetation, flycatchers, doves, Galápagos hawks, and mockingbirds are evident in the inland regions, and several types of shorebirds continue to flourish at Puerto Egas.

View north across James Bay from atop Sugarloaf volcano. A three-hundred-year-old lava flow separates
Puerto Egas from Espumilla Beach at the northern end
of James Bay. The road from an old salt mine leading
from the small spatter cone at the right of the photograph is visible.

View up to Sugarloaf from Puerto Egas. The open
grassy landscape is partly a result of the large population of feral goats, which devour native species of
plants. The young prickly pear cactus is heavily armored with spines, but becomes less "prickly" as it
grows older, at which point it becomes threatened by
goats. A small spring on the side of the volcano attracts
many kinds of birds as well as goats.

Tuffstone formations on the shoreline create striking "caves" for lounging female sea lions. Here, the view is shown from both sides of the rock. On the left, the slopes of Sugarloaf interrupt the ashy layers.

View into the crater of Sugarloaf, brush-stroked with lava, from its highest northwestern point. The island of Ráb-ida can be seen in the distance.

Fernandina

FORBIDDEN REFUGE

A vivid pioneering species of lava cactus, the *Brachycereus*, begins its colonization of the "ropy" lava at Punta Espinosa. The rounded outline of Fernandina's shield volcano rises 5,000 feet in the distance.

With its dark, rocky shores, black sand beaches, and frequent volcanic upheavals, Fernandina, west of Isabela, seems in many ways the most forbidding and yet the most fascinating of the Galápagos islands. Its wildlife reflects Fernandina's primeval character. Like hundreds of small dragons, enormous armies of marine iguanas guard the coastlines, in particular at Punta Espinosa, at the northeastern edge of the island. These creatures are the only known lizards to have adapted themselves to a life dependent on the sea, feeding on the green algae that blooms in the intertidal areas and on the lush carpet of seaweed several feet below the water's surface. A vast array of animal life, comparatively rarely touched by human contact, thrives in these nutrient-laden waters, and the profiles of the endemic flightless cormorant, with its ancient-looking ragged wings, Galápagos penguins, and sea lions can be distinguished among the rocks. Punta Espinosa is rimmed at its base with a forest of green mangroves and a wide swath of lava and shell sand. On other parts of the coastline, such as in the waters surrounding Cape Douglas, fur seals are found. No introduced or feral animals roam here, making species that survive only in small numbers or not at all on other islands, like the iguanas and the small native rice rat, common. Fernandina also boasts a large population of land iguanas, although the favored nesting ground of these lizards, the rim of the single volcano's caldera, has been destroyed by recent eruptions.

Fernandina is the newest of the Galápagos volcanos, with the exception of the Volcán Chico area of Sierra Negra on Isabela, and it remains one of the most active. Its youth is evident in its lack of signs of erosion and its bareness of vegetation, and from the sea it looms like a large, rounded shadow. Near the coast its slope is gentle, but inland the mountain gradually steepens, rising to some 4,900 feet before it levels out at the rim of the 3,000-foot-deep caldera. Fernandina has erupted several times in the last few decades. The majority of the eruptions were of fluid basaltic lavas, which flowed down the inside of the caldera, but the most dramatic explosion occurred in 1968, when the caldera floor itself dropped by almost a thousand feet, producing hundreds of earthquakes and sending up a tall pillar of ash, which traveled for many miles. The lake in the caldera has also led an unsettled life, changing positions from one side of the crater to the other—a result of crustal shifts—and even disappearing twice, most recently with the eruption of the volcano in September 1988.

Galápagos fur seals (upper and lower left) are smaller and stockier than their nearest relatives, the California sea lions. Fur seals are actually a type of sea lion (rather than seals) as they have visible ears and use their front flippers for swimming and for propping themselves up on land. The fur seal's double-layered coat (visible in the lower left photograph) was highly prized during the nineteenth century and attracted many sealers to the archipelago. Tens of thousands of seals were taken and the fur seal was hunted almost to extinction. With protection, their numbers have recovered. The Galápagos subspecies of the California sea lion (upper and lower right) is found on the beaches and gently sloping rocky coasts of many of the islands. They are larger, sleeker, and possess a more pointed face than fur seals. Sea lion pups are known for their exceptionally playful nature.

OPPOSITE:
Sea lions relax by a tidepool at sunset on Punta Espinosa.

Despite being unable to fly, the flightless cormorant still dries its rudimentary wings after swimming. The only living cormorant that has lost its ability to fly, this bird, endemic to the Galápagos, is of special interest to conservationists. The current population is restricted to the shores of Fernandina and the western regions of Isabela.

The adult flightless cormorant has a jewel-like turquoise-blue eye that contrasts with its otherwise dull plumage. The hooked tip of the bird's bill is well-adapted to pulling eels and octopi from underwater crevices for food.

A pair of American oystercatchers at Punta Espinosa. Some two hundred pairs of oystercatchers are resident in the Galápagos. Extraordinarily tame in the islands because of their lack of native predators, the birds forage along the shores for shellfish, oblivious to the occasional human intrusion.

Nesting flightless cormorants silhouetted against the sky. After a complex courtship and mating pattern, most of which occurs in the water, these birds will build large nests of out of seaweed on the lava, in which they will raise two or three young.

A colony of marine iguanas appears to almost pave the jagged rocks at Punta Espinosa. The only sea-going lizard in existence, the marine iguana feeds on algae and seaweed found in shallow reef areas and regions where there are large expanses of intertidal zone such as on Fernandina.

Intertidal zone, Punta Espinosa, with a view across the Bolivar Channel to Volcán Darwin, on the island of Isabela, only five miles away.

OVERLEAF:
The marine iguanas of Fernandina are among the largest in the Galápagos. During the peak sun hours, this jumble of dark shapes, which seem to be part of the landscape, will assume an orderly arrangement—oriented toward the sun for optimum basking.

A bush of bright green *Scalesia affinis* finds a suitable microclimate for growth inside a lava collapse. The collapse will provide moisture and protection from drying winds for the plant in an otherwise inhospitable black desert.

Looking down the buckled-lava encrusted flanks of Fernandina's main volcano.

The tails of land iguanas have traced fragile trails around a nest burrow. A few footprints can also be seen. Fernandina boasts one of the largest undisturbed populations of land iguanas in the archipelago, and its soft, sandy ash deposits permit easy digging by the iguanas. A number of these nesting sites were destroyed by recent volcanic eruption, seriously affecting the land iguana population.

A land iguana's yellow-brown coloration contrasts dramatically with Fernandina's volcanic rim.

The view into Fernandina's caldera does not remain the same for long. The black lava flows evident have all occurred since the floor of the caldera fell by 1,000 feet in 1968 during volcanic activity, swallowing the lake. A 1988 eruption of the volcano once again caused the lake to disappear. This photograph was one of the last to be taken of the lake. The large cone near the lake is now covered with avalanches of debris that resulted from the collapsing crater wall.

A pit crater—perhaps more than 1,000 feet deep despite its small diameter—shows a cross section of lava layers near Fernandina's volcanic rim.

Bartolomé and Sulivan Bay EARTHLY MOONSCAPE

Pinnacle Rock stands sentinel on the island of Bartolomé, with Cerro Inn, a large ash cone on the island of Santiago, in the background.

A small rugged island off the eastern shore of Santiago, Bartolomé lies opposite Sulivan Bay. The area of Sulivan Bay, a cascade of lava, punctuated at water's edge with fine white sand, was formed by the flow from a nearby shield volcano that erupted at the turn of this century. (The present Sulivan Bay was not in existence when James Sulivan, from whom the bay takes its name, visited the Galápagos as second lieutenant aboard HMS *Beagle* with Charles Darwin.) Together, Bartolomé and Sulivan Bay evoke a lunar landscape of cones and craters in varying shades of deep chocolate and light brown, black, and gray.

The guardian point of Pinnacle Rock on Bartolomé, the worn-away remnant of a cone composed of spewed ashy particles, is one of the best-known landmarks in the archipelago. A stretch of land on the western part of the island is notched out on both sides by coral-sand beaches (the north shore a popular swimming and snorkeling site), around which flourish lush mangroves and other salt-tolerant plant life. Away from the water, however, Bartolomé is stark and dry, and only the occasional prickly pear, lava cactus, or *Scalesia* bush has managed to survive among the spatter cones and lava tubes (the crusted-over "tunnels," now empty, through which volumes of molten rock once raced). Climbing the island's summit trail reveals a peculiar adaptation to the environment, the *Tequilia* plant, which at first glance looks like dead brush but which is actually made up of leaves covered with tiny gray hairs that help prevent the evaporation of moisture caused by the desiccating winds and reflect the unremitting sunlight. A range of wildlife thrives where the landscape is more forgiving: the diminutive Galápagos penguins are frequently seen, and a small cave behind Pinnacle Rock houses a breeding colony. Green sea turtles and herons make use of the gentler beaches.

The lava flow at Sulivan Bay is one of the finest examples of the rope-like *pahohoe* lava, which has oozed over older flows, resulting in fascinating buckled patterns and a palette of colors from fresh hot material rushing over and around older, hardened lavas. In some places, the most recent flow has engulfed small trees, burning and destroying them but cooling the lava enough to leave a virtual mold of their bark and other features. Scattered vegetation has begun to colonize the new flow, now about ninety years old, and in the cracks and crevices one may find the intrepid lava cactus or a wispy *Mollugo* plant.

149

Century-old lava flow at Sulivan Bay, Santiago, is an arresting example of the wrinkled *pahoehoe* lava. *Pahoehoe* is the Hawaiian word for "ropy" (the Hawaiian islands, like the Galápagos, are oceanic volcanoes and exhibit similar geological features). The small hills in the distance are the eroded remnants of old cinder cones.

The fluid-looking patterns of the *pahoehoe* lava flow at Sulivan Bay are the result of volcanic upheavals during which still molten lava continues to move under the partly solidified skin-like crust, "freezing" it in motion for years to come.

The almost lunar appearance of the ashy slopes of Bartolomé come from the pale gray *Tiquilia* plants, and the lava boulders tumbled from the spatter cones farther up, that scatter the volcano's flanks.

OVERLEAF:
New meets old. Opposite, new lava has surrounded and partly coats a fragment of an older cinder cone. The fragment probably was broken off by the flowing lava and then carried some distance like a log in a stream. At right, tongues of fresh black lava lap the brown slopes of a much older cinder cone. Pinnacle Rock can be seen in the distance.

PAGES 156–57:
Steep-sided spatter cones, formed as lava is ejected from volcanic vents, stud the flanks of Bartolomé against a backdrop that includes the Sulivan Bay lava flow and Bainbridge Rocks.

153

ABOVE:

A Sally lightfoot, or red lava, crab moves over a tidal rock in search of small bits of plant or animal life for food. Found throughout the Galápagos as well as at Sulivan Bay, this crab is named for its ability to scuttle rapidly over the surface of a tidepool without sinking. While the adult lightfoots are bright red, the young are black, blending into the landscape.

RIGHT:

Sea lions enjoy the surf at Sulivan Bay beach, guarded by Pinnacle Rock. The clear white sand, composed of shell and coral particles, contrasts starkly with the surrounding lava shores.

OVERLEAF:

Surf rolls up on the south beach of Bartolomé. Small white-tipped sharks can often be seen swimming close by, and green sea turtles find this a favorite nesting beach.

Acknowledgments

Many people have helped me to realize this project. My sincere thanks goes to the entire staff of the Charles Darwin Research Station on Santa Cruz, especially Sylvia Harcourt; Gunther Reck, director; Alfredo Carrasco; Fausto Valencia; Luis Ramos; and Hank Kasteleign. The guides with whom I worked were always excellent: their love of and sensitivity to the natural environment were an inspiration. Freddy Perez and ''Bosco'' also cheerfully carried large amounts of equipment. Gil De Roy—an extraordinary guide and naturalist—grew up in the Galápagos, and his knowledge and willingness to share it all will never be forgotten. Heinz and Irene Schatz, while not official guides, gave me invaluable assistance at Alcedo. I also want to express my appreciation to the director of the Galápagos National Park, Humberto Ochoa Cordova, for his help.

A number of people in the United States were important to the production of this book. The staff of Laumont Color Laboratory—particularly Ben Pelez—an Ecuadorian—worked with great care to ensure that each sheet of film received exacting processing. Ruth Sergel and Israel Rosenzweig accompanied me to the Galápagos as my able assistants. Their effort and organizational skills left me free to concentrate on making photographs. Betty Marks, my agent, has been a continual source of encouragement and a good friend well beyond her professional role. Working with the designer Nai Chang has once again been a genuine pleasure; and Stephanie Salomon, my editor, has contributed tremendously in shaping this publication.

Select Bibliography

Beebe, William. GALAPAGOS—WORLD'S END. New York: C.P. Putnam and Sons, 1924.

Brower, K, and E. Porter. THE FLOW OF WILDNESS. San Francisco: Sierra Club and Ballantine Books, 1968.

Darwin, Charles. THE VOYAGE OF THE BEAGLE. Doubleday and Co.: Garden City, New York, 1962.

———. ON THE ORIGIN OF SPECIES. New York: Atheneum Press, 1967.

Harris, M. A FIELD GUIDE TO THE BIRDS OF THE GALAPAGOS. London: Collins, 1974.

Hickin, N. ANIMAL LIFE OF THE GALAPAGOS. Quito, Ecuador: Libri Mundi, 1979.

Hickman, John. THE ENCHANTED ISLANDS—THE GALAPAGOS DISCOVERED. Oswestry, England: Anthony Nelson, 1985.

Jackson, M.H. GALAPAGOS: A NATURAL HISTORY GUIDE. Calgary: University of Calgary Press, 1985.

Moore, Tui de Roy. GALAPAGOS: ISLANDS LOST IN TIME. New York: Viking Press, 1980.

Nelson, J.B. GALAPAGOS: ISLANDS OF BIRDS. London: Longmans, Green; New York: Morrow, 1968.

Perry, R. THE GALAPAGOS ISLANDS. New York: Dodd, Mead, 1972.

———, ed. GALAPAGOS—KEY ENVIRONMENTS. Oxford, England: Pergamon Press, 1984.

Steadman, David W., and Steven Zousmer. GALAPAGOS: DISCOVERY ON DARWIN'S ISLANDS. Washington, D.C.: Smithsonian Institution Press, 1988.

White, Alan, and Bruce Epler. GALAPAGOS GUIDE. Quito, Ecuador: Libri Mundi, 1985.